VEGAN BURGERS & SANDWICHES PART.1

CLOE BERZ

VEGAN BURGERS & SANDWICHES PART.1
by CLOE BERZ

INTRODUCTION

The U.S. has the largest fast food industry in the world, and there are American fast food restaurants in over 100 countries. People of all kinds are drawn to the low-cost, high-speed restaurants that serve indulgent and popular foods.

But let's be honest, the food is hardly healthy. The good news is that it's easy to make your favorite fast food menu items at home. You get to choose the ingredients so they can be healthy as well as nostalgic and indulgent.

You like burgers, sandwiches, tacos, empanadas, and burritos and you're looking for vegan versions? Then you will love this roundup of drool-worthy vegan fast food recipes!

SANDWICHES AND WRAPS

a. Tempeh Reuben Sandwiches

Makes 2 sandwiches

- 8 ounces tempeh

- 3 tablespoons vegan mayonnaise, homemade (see Vegan Mayonnaise) or store-bought

- 1 tablespoon sweet pickle relish

- 1 green onion, minced

- 2 tablespoons olive oil

- Salt and freshly ground black pepper
- 1

- 4 slices rye or pumpernickel bread

- $\frac{3}{4}$ cup sauerkraut, well drained

In a medium saucepan of simmering water, cook the tempeh for 30 minutes. Drain the tempeh and set aside to cool. Pat dry and cut into $1/4$-inch slices.

In a small bowl, combine the mayonnaise, ketchup, relish, and green onion. Season with salt and pepper to taste, blend well, and set aside.

In a medium skillet, heat the oil over medium heat. Add the tempeh and cook until golden brown on both sides, about 10 minutes total. Season with salt and pepper to taste. Remove from the skillet and set aside.

Wipe out the skillet and set aside. Spread margarine on one side of each slice of bread. Place 2 slices of bread, margarine side down, in the skillet. Spread the dressing onto both slices of bread and layer with the fried tempeh and the sauerkraut.

Top each with the remaining 2 slices of bread, margarine side up. Transfer the sandwiches to the skillet and cook until lightly browned on both sides, turning once, about 2 minutes per side.

Remove the sandwiches from the skillet, cut in half, and serve immediately.

2. Portobello Po'Boys

Makes 4 po'boys

- 3 tablespoons olive oil

- 4 portobello mushroom caps, lightly rinsed, patted dry, and cut into 1-inch pieces

- 1 teaspoon Cajun seasoning

- Salt and freshly ground black pepper

- $1/4$ cup vegan mayonnaise, homemade (see Vegan Mayonnaise) or store-bought

- 4 crusty sandwich rolls, halved horizontally

- 4 slices ripe tomato

- $1^1/2$ cups shredded romaine lettuce

- Tabasco sauce

In a large skillet, heat the oil over medium heat. Add the mushrooms and cook until browned and softened, about 8 minutes. Season with the Cajun seasoning and salt and pepper to taste. Set aside.

Spread mayonnaise onto the cut sides of each of the rolls. Place a tomato slice on the bottom of each roll, top with shredded lettuce. Arrange the mushroom pieces on top, sprinkle with Tabasco to taste, top with the other half of the roll, and serve.

Shake Up Your Sandwich Routine

Whether we're packing a school lunch for the kids or brown bagging our own lunch for work, many of us get into a sandwich rut. After all, how can you improve on a good PB&J? It's fast, easy, and economical. But everyone likes a little variety now and then, and when you begin to think outside the lunchbox, the possibilities for variation become endless.

Much in the way the right accessories can make a great outfit, it's often the little touches that make a great sandwich. Here are some ways to shake up your sandwich routine:

Do a bread swap: If you normally ensconce your burger in a bun, try it in a wrap. If that hummus spread is always in a pita, try it on two slabs of pumpernickel.

Change your condiments: Try a new spicy mustard or add some curry or wasabi to your vegan mayo. Use a chutney or relish instead of ketchup on your veggie burger. You'll be amazed how the same old sandwich suddenly tastes brand-new.

Add a layer: If it's a PB&J, add a layer of fresh or dried fruit, chopped nuts, or even minced celery or shredded carrot. Yum's the word. For a burger or other "meaty" sandwich like seitan or tempeh, add a layer of grilled or roasted veggies such as thinly sliced zucchini, bell pepper, mushroom, or onion.

Turn over a new leaf: Still using iceberg on your sandwiches after all these years? Slide in a leaf of soft butter lettuce, crunchy romaine, or peppery arugula. Worried about wilting? Pack the lettuce separately in a zip-top bag and tuck it into your sandwich when it's time to eat.

On the side: Even a sandwich deserves good company. Bring along a side of slaw, bean salad, potato salad, or fruit salad. And don't forget the pickles and chips.

3. Tastes like Tuna Salad Sandwiches

Makes 4 sandwiches

- $1\frac{1}{2}$ cups cooked or 1 (15.5-ounce) can chickpeas, drained and rinsed

- 2 celery ribs, minced

- $\frac{1}{4}$ cup minced onion

- 1 teaspoon capers, drained and chopped

- 1 cup vegan mayonnaise, homemade (see [Vegan Mayonnaise](#)) or store-bought, divided

- 2 teaspoons fresh lemon juice

- 1 teaspoon Dijon mustard

- 1 teaspoon kelp powder

- 4 lettuce leaves

- 4 slices ripe tomato

- Salt and pepper

- Bread

In a medium bowl, coarsely mash the chickpeas. Add the celery, onion, capers, $1/2$ cup of the mayonnaise, lemon juice, mustard, and kelp powder. Season with salt and pepper to taste. Mix until well combined. Cover and refrigerate at least 30 minutes to allow flavors to blend.

When ready to serve, spread the remaining $1/4$ cup mayonnaise onto 1 side of each of the bread slices. Layer lettuce and tomato on 4 of the bread slices and evenly divide the chickpea mixture among them. Top each sandwich with the remaining slice of bread, mayonnaise side down, cut in half, and serve.

4. Sloppy Bulgur Sandwiches

Makes 4 sandwiches

- 1¾ cups water

- 1 cup medium-grind bulgur

- Salt

- 1 tablespoon olive oil

- 1 small red onion, minced

- ¹/₂ medium red bell pepper, minced

- (14.5-ounce) can crushed tomatoes

- 1 tablespoon sugar

- 1 tablespoon yellow or spicy brown mustard

- 2 teaspoons soy sauce

- 1 teaspoon chili powder

- Freshly ground black pepper

- 4 sandwich rolls, halved horizontally

In a large saucepan, bring the water to boil over high heat. Stir in the bulgur and lightly salt the water. Cover, remove from heat, and set aside until the bulgur softens and the water is absorbed, about 20 minutes.

Meanwhile, in a large skillet, heat the oil over medium heat. Add the onion and bell pepper, cover, and cook until soft, about 7 minutes. Stir in the tomatoes, sugar, mustard, soy sauce, chili powder, and salt and black pepper to taste. Simmer for 10 minutes, stirring frequently.

Spoon the bulgur mixture onto the bottom half of each of the rolls, top with the other half, and serve.

5. Curried Tofu "Egg Salad" Pitas

Makes 4 sandwiches

- 1 pound extra-firm tofu, drained and patted dry

- $^1/_2$ cup vegan mayonnaise, homemade (see Vegan Mayonnaise) or store-bought

- $1/4$ cup chopped mango chutney, homemade (see Mango Chutney) or store-bought

- 2 teaspoons Dijon mustard

- 1 tablespoon hot or mild curry powder

- 1 teaspoon salt

- $1/8$ teaspoon ground cayenne

- 1 cup shredded carrots

- 2 celery ribs, minced

- $1/4$ cup minced red onion

- 8 small Boston or other soft lettuce leaves

- 4 (7-inch) whole wheat pita breads, halved

Crumble the tofu and place it in a large bowl. Add the mayonnaise, chutney, mustard, curry powder, salt, and cayenne, and stir well until thoroughly mixed.

Add the carrots, celery, and onion and stir to combine. Refrigerate for 30 minutes to allow the flavors to blend.

Tuck a lettuce leaf inside each pita pocket, spoon some tofu mixture on top of the lettuce, and serve.

6. Garden Patch Sandwiches on Bread

Makes 4 sandwiches

- 1 pound extra-firm tofu, drained and patted dry

- 1 medium red bell pepper, finely chopped

- 1 celery rib, finely chopped

- 3 green onions, minced

- $1/4$ cup shelled sunflower seeds

- $1/2$ cup vegan mayonnaise, homemade (see Vegan Mayonnaise) or store-bought

- $1/2$ teaspoon salt

- $1/2$ teaspoon celery salt

- $1/4$ teaspoon freshly ground black pepper

- 8 slices whole grain bread

- ($1/4$-inch) slices ripe tomato

- lettuce leaves

Crumble the tofu and place it in a large bowl. Add the bell pepper, celery, green onions, and sunflower seeds. Stir in the mayonnaise, salt, celery salt, and pepper and mix until well combined.

Toast the bread, if desired. Spread the mixture evenly onto 4 slices of the bread. Top each with a tomato slice, lettuce leaf, and the remaining bread. Cut the sandwiches diagonally in half and serve.

7. Fruit-And-Nut Sandwiches

Makes 4 sandwiches

- $^2/_3$ cup almond butter

- $^1/_4$ cup agave nectar or pure maple syrup

- $^1/_4$ cup chopped walnuts or other nuts of choice

- $^1/_4$ cup sweetened dried cranberries

- 8 slices whole grain bread

- 2 ripe Bosc or Anjou pears, cored and thinly sliced

In a small bowl, combine the almond butter, agave nectar, walnuts, and cranberries, stirring until well mixed.

Divide the mixture among the bread slices and spread evenly. Top 4 slices of the bread with the pear slices, spread side up. Place the remaining slices of bread on top of the pear slices, spread side down. Slice the sandwiches diagonally and serve at once.

8. Marinated Mushroom Wraps

Makes 2 wraps

- 3 tablespoons soy sauce

- 3 tablespoons fresh lemon juice

- $1^1/_2$ tablespoons toasted sesame oil

- 2 portobello mushroom caps, cut into $^1/_4$-inch strips

- 1 ripe Hass avocado, pitted and peeled

- (10-inch) flour tortillas

- 2 cups fresh baby spinach leaves

- 1 medium red bell pepper, cut into $^1/_4$-inch strips

- 1 ripe tomato, chopped

- Salt and freshly ground black pepper

In a medium bowl, combine the soy sauce, 2 tablespoons of the lemon juice, and the oil. Add the portobello strips, toss to combine, and marinate for 1 hour or overnight. Drain the mushrooms and set aside.

Mash the avocado with the remaining 1 tablespoon of lemon juice.

To assemble wraps, place 1 tortilla on a work surface and spread with some of the mashed avocado. Top with a layer of baby spinach leaves. In the lower third of each tortilla, arrange strips of the soaked mushrooms and some of the bell pepper strips. Sprinkle with the tomato and salt and black pepper to taste. Roll up tightly and cut in half diagonally. Repeat with the remaining ingredients and serve.

9. Peanutty Tofu Roll-Ups

Makes 4 wraps

- 8 ounces extra-firm tofu, drained well and patted dry
- 1 tablespoon soy sauce
- 1 tablespoon fresh lime juice
- $1/2$ teaspoon grated fresh ginger

- 1 garlic clove, minced

- $1/4$ teaspoon ground cayenne

- 4 (10-inch) flour tortillas or lavash flatbread

- 2 cups shredded romaine lettuce

- 1 large carrot, grated

- $1/2$ medium English cucumber, peeled and cut into $1/4$-inch slices

In a food processor, combine the tofu, peanut butter, and soy sauce and process until smooth. Add the lime juice, ginger, garlic, and cayenne and process until smooth. Set aside for 30 minutes at room temperature to allow flavors to blend.

To assemble wraps, place 1 tortilla on a work surface and spread with about $1/2$ cup of the tofu

mixture. Sprinkle with lettuce, carrot, and cucumber. Roll up tightly and cut in half diagonally. Repeat with the remaining ingredients and serve.

10.   Garden Salad Wraps

Makes 4 wraps

- 6 tablespoons olive oil

- 1 pound extra-firm tofu, drained, patted dry, and cut into $1/2$-inch strips

- 1 tablespoon soy sauce

- $1/4$ cup apple cider vinegar

- 1 teaspoon yellow or spicy brown mustard

- $1/2$ teaspoon salt

- $1/4$ teaspoon freshly ground black pepper

- 3 cups shredded romaine lettuce

- 3 ripe Roma tomatoes, finely chopped

- 1 large carrot, shredded

- 1 medium English cucumber, peeled and chopped

- $1/3$ cup minced red onion

- $1/4$ cup sliced pitted green olives

- 4 (10-inch) flour tortillas or lavash flatbread

In a large skillet, heat 2 tablespoons of the oil over medium heat. Add the tofu and cook until golden brown, about 10 minutes. Sprinkle with soy sauce and set aside to cool.

In a small bowl, combine the vinegar, mustard, salt, and pepper with the remaining 4 tablespoons oil, stirring to blend well. Set aside.

In a large bowl, combine the lettuce, tomatoes, carrot, cucumber, onion, and olives. Pour on the dressing and toss to coat.

To assemble wraps, place 1 tortilla on a work surface and spread with about one-quarter of the salad. Place a few strips of tofu on the tortilla and roll up tightly. Slice in half diagonally. Repeat with remaining ingredients and serve.

11.   Tempeh-Walnut Salad Wraps

Makes 4 wraps

- 8 ounces tempeh

- $1/2$ cup chopped walnuts

- 1 celery rib, chopped

- $1/4$ cup finely chopped green onions

- $1/4$ cup finely chopped red bell pepper

- 2 tablespoons minced fresh parsley

- 1 cup vegan mayonnaise, homemade (see Vegan Mayonnaise) or store-bought, divided

- 1 tablespoon Dijon mustard

- 1 teaspoon fresh lemon juice

- $1/2$ teaspoon salt

- $1/8$ teaspoon freshly ground black pepper

- 4 (10-inch) tortillas or lavash flatbread

- 1 to 2 cups shredded romaine lettuce

In a medium saucepan of simmering water, cook the tempeh for 30 minutes. Remove tempeh from pan and set aside to cool.

Pat the tempeh dry, chop it finely, and place it in a bowl. Add the walnuts, celery, green onions, bell pepper, and parsley. Stir in $1/2$ cup of the mayonnaise, the mustard, lemon juice, salt, and black pepper. Mix until thoroughly combined.

Cover and refrigerate at least 30 minutes to allow flavors to blend. Taste, adjusting seasonings if necessary.

To assemble wraps, place 1 tortilla on a work surface and spread with 1 tablespoon of the remaining mayonnaise. Top with about $^2/_3$ cup of the tempeh mixture. Top with shredded lettuce and roll up tightly. Cut each tortilla in half diagonally. Repeat with remaining ingredients.

12.   Avocado And Tempeh Wraps

Makes 4 wraps

- 2 tablespoons olive oil

- 8 ounces tempeh bacon, homemade (see
  Tempeh Bacon) or store-bought

- 4 (10-inch) soft flour tortillas or lavash flat
  bread

- $1/4$ cup vegan mayonnaise, homemade (see [Vegan Mayonnaise](#)) or store-bought

- 4 large lettuce leaves

- 2 ripe Hass avocados, pitted, peeled, and cut into $1/4$-inch slices

In a large skillet, heat the oil over medium heat. Add the tempeh bacon and cook until browned on both sides, about 8 minutes. Remove from the heat and set aside.

Place 1 tortilla on a work surface. Spread with some of the mayonnaise and one-fourth of the lettuce and tomatoes.

Pit, peel, and thinly slice the avocado and place the slices on top of the tomato. Add the reserved tempeh bacon and roll up tightly. Repeat with remaining ingredients and serve.

13. Chickpea-Tomato Wraps

Makes 4 wraps

- $1^1/_2$ cups cooked or 1 (15.5-ounce) cans chickpeas, drained and rinsed
- 1 celery rib, minced
- $^1/_4$ cup minced red onion
- 3 tablespoons chopped fresh parsley

- $^1/_2$ cup vegan mayonnaise, homemade (see Vegan Mayonnaise) or store-bought

- 1 tablespoon spicy brown mustard

- Salt and freshly ground black pepper

- 4 (10-inch) flour tortillas or lavash flatbread

- 4 lettuce leaves

Mash the chickpeas in a large bowl. Cut the tomatoes into $^1/_4$-inch pieces and add to the chickpeas

along with the celery, onion, and parsley. Add the mayonnaise, mustard, and salt and pepper to taste, stirring to mix well.

To assemble wraps, place 1 tortilla on a work surface and spread about $^1/_2$ cup of the chickpea

mixture across the surface. Top with a lettuce leaf. Roll up tightly and cut in half diagonally. Repeat with the remaining ingredients and serve.

*To use dried sun-dried tomatoes, place them in a heatproof bowl and cover with boiling water. Set aside 10 minutes to reconstitute.

14.　　Tofu Waldorf Salad Wraps

Makes 4 wraps

- 1 pound extra-firm tofu, drained, patted dry, and cut in $^{1}/_{2}$-inch dice

- 2 firm crisp apples, such as Gala or Fuji, cored and chopped

- 2 celery ribs, minced

- $1/3$ minced red onion

- $1/3$ cup chopped walnuts, toasted

- 2 tablespoons chopped fresh parsley

- $1/2$ cup vegan mayonnaise, homemade (see Vegan Mayonnaise) or store-bought

- 2 tablespoons fresh lemon juice

- $1/2$ teaspoon sugar

- $1/2$ teaspoon salt

- $1/4$ teaspoon freshly ground black pepper

- 4 (10-inch) flour tortillas or lavash flatbread

- 4 lettuce leaves

In a large bowl, combine the tofu, apples, celery, onion, walnuts, and parsley. Add the mayonnaise, lemon juice, sugar, salt, and pepper, stirring well to combine.

To assemble wraps, lay 1 tortilla on a work surface. Spread about $^1/_2$ cup of the tofu mixture

across the tortilla and top with a lettuce leaf. Roll up tightly and cut in half diagonally. Repeat with the remaining ingredients and serve.

15. Teriyaki Tofu Wraps

Makes 4 wraps

- 3 tablespoons soy sauce

- 1 tablespoon fresh lemon juice

- 1 tablespoon sugar

- 1 garlic clove, minced

- 2 tablespoons toasted sesame oil

- $1/4$ teaspoon ground cayenne

- 1 pound extra-firm tofu, drained, patted dry, and cut into $1/2$-inch strips

- 2 tablespoons olive oil

- 1 large red bell pepper, cut into $1/4$-inch strips

- 4 (10-inch) flour tortillas or lavash flatbread, warmed

In a small bowl, combine the soy sauce, lemon juice, sugar, garlic, sesame oil, and cayenne and set aside.

Place the tofu in a shallow bowl. Pour the teriyaki marinade over the tofu, turning gently to coat.

In a large skillet, heat the oil over medium heat. Remove the tofu from the marinade, reserving the marinade. Place the tofu in the hot skillet along with the bell pepper and cook until the tofu is browned and the peppers are tender, about 10 minutes. Pour the reserved marinade over the tofu and peppers and simmer, stirring gently to coat.

To assemble wraps, place 1 tortilla on a work surface and place some of the tofu and pepper strips across the lower third. Roll up tightly. Repeat with remaining ingredients and serve.

16.   Tofu-Tahini Veggie Wraps

Makes 4 wraps

- 8 ounces extra-firm tofu, drained and patted dry

- 3 green onions, minced

- 2 celery ribs, minced

- $^1/_2$ cup minced fresh parsley

- 2 tablespoons capers

- 2 tablespoons fresh lemon juice

- 1 tablespoon Dijon mustard

- $1/2$ teaspoon salt

- $1/8$ teaspoon ground cayenne

- 4 (10-inch) flour tortillas or lavash

- 1 medium carrot, shredded

- 4 lettuce leaves

In a food processor, combine the tofu, tahini, green onions, celery, parsley, capers, lemon juice, mustard, salt, and cayenne and process until well combined.

To assemble wraps, place 1 tortilla on a work surface and spread about $1/2$ cup of the tofu mixture across the tortilla. Sprinkle with shredded carrot and top with a lettuce leaf. Roll up tightly and cut in half diagonally. Repeat with the remaining ingredients and serve.

17.   Deconstructed Hummus Pitas

Makes 4 pitas

- 1 garlic clove, crushed

- ¾ cup tahini (sesame paste)

- 2 tablespoons fresh lemon juice

- 1 teaspoon salt

- $1/8$ teaspoon ground cayenne

- $^1/_4$ cup water

- $1^1/_2$ cups cooked or 1 (15.5-ounce) can chickpeas, rinsed and drained

- 2 medium carrots, grated (about 1 cup)

- 4 (7-inch) pita breads, preferably whole wheat, halved

- 2 cups fresh baby spinach

In a blender or food processor, mince the garlic. Add the tahini, lemon juice, salt, cayenne, and water. Process until smooth.

Place the chickpeas in a bowl and crush slightly with a fork. Add the carrots and the reserved tahini sauce and toss to combine. Set aside.

Spoon 2 or 3 tablespoons of the chickpea mixture into each pita half. Tuck a tomato slice and a few spinach leaves into each pocket and serve.

18.   Muffaletta Sandwiches

Makes 4 sandwiches

- 1 cup chopped pitted kalamata olives

- 1 cup chopped pimiento-stuffed green olives

- $^1/_2$ cup chopped pepperoncini (pickled peppers)

- $1/2$ cup jarred roasted red peppers (or see Roasted Red Pepper Hummus), chopped

- 2 tablespoons capers

- 3 green onions, minced

- 3 plum tomatoes, chopped

- 2 tablespoons minced fresh parsley

- $1/2$ teaspoon dried marjoram

- $1/2$ teaspoon dried thyme

- $1/4$ cup olive oil

- 2 tablespoons white wine vinegar

- Salt and freshly ground black pepper

- 4 individual kaiser rolls, boules, or other crusty sandwich rolls, halved horizontally

In a medium bowl, combine the kalamata olives, green olives, pepperoncini, red peppers, capers, green onions, tomatoes, parsley, marjoram, thyme, oil, vinegar, and salt and black pepper to taste. Set aside.

Pull out some of the inside of the sandwich rolls to make room for the filling. Spoon the filling mixture into the bottom half of the rolls, packing lightly. Top with remaining roll halves and serve.

19. Falafel Sandwiches

Makes 4 sandwiches

- $1^1/_2$ cups cooked or 1 (15.5-ounce) can chickpeas, drained and rinsed

- 3 garlic cloves, chopped

- 1 small yellow onion, chopped

- 3 tablespoons chopped fresh parsley

- $^1/_2$ cup old-fashioned oats

- 1 teaspoon ground cumin

- 1 teaspoon ground coriander

- 1 teaspoon salt

- $^1/_4$ teaspoon freshly ground black pepper

- Chickpea flour or all-purpose flour, for dredging

- Olive oil, for frying

- 4 loaves pita bread, cut in half

- Shredded romaine lettuce, to serve

- 1 ripe tomato, chopped

- $^1/_2$ cup Tahini-Lemon Sauce

In a food processor, combine the chickpeas, garlic, onion, parsley, oats, cumin, coriander, salt, and pepper and process to combine. Refrigerate for 20 to 30 minutes.

Form the mixture into small balls, about 2 inches in diameter. If the mixture is not firm enough, add up to $1/4$ cup of flour, a little at a time, until the desired consistency is reached. Flatten the balls into patties and dredge them in flour.

In a large skillet, heat a thin layer of oil over medium-high heat. Add the falafel and cook, turning once, until golden brown, about 8 minutes total.

Stuff the falafel patties into the pita pockets, along with lettuce, tomato, and tahini sauce. Serve immediately.

20.   Vietnamese Po'Boys

Makes 4 po'boys

- 1 tablespoon canola or grapeseed oil

- 1 recipe Soy-Tan Dream Cutlets

- 2 tablespoons soy sauce

- 2 teaspoons Asian chili sauce (such as Sriracha)

- 3 tablespoons vegan mayonnaise, homemade (see Vegan Mayonnaise) or store-bought

- 2 teaspoons fresh lime juice

- (7-inch) baguettes, split lengthwise

- $1/2$ small red onion, thinly sliced

- 1 medium carrot, shredded

- $1/2$ medium English cucumber, cut into $1/4$-inch slices

- $1/2$ cup fresh cilantro leaves

- 1 tablespoon minced jalapeño (optional)

In a skillet, heat the oil over medium heat. Add the soy-tan cutlets and cook until browned on both sides, turning once, about 8 minutes total.

About halfway through, sprinkle the cutlets with the soy sauce and 1 teaspoon of the chili sauce. Set aside to cool to room temperature.

In a small bowl, combine the remaining chili sauce with the mayonnaise and lime juice, stirring to blend well.

Spread the mayonnaise mixture onto the inside of the baguettes. Layer with the onion, carrot, cucumber, cilantro, and jalapeño, if using. Thinly slice the reserved soy-tan cutlets and arrange the slices on top. Serve immediately.

BURGERS

21.   Tempeh Tantrum Burgers

Makes 4 burgers

- 8 ounces tempeh, cut into $^1/_2$-inch dice

- $\frac{3}{4}$ cup chopped onion

- 2 garlic cloves, chopped

- $\frac{3}{4}$ cup chopped walnuts

- $^1/_2$ cup old-fashioned or quick-cooking oats

- 1 tablespoon minced fresh parsley

- $\frac{1}{2}$ teaspoon dried oregano

- $\frac{1}{2}$ teaspoon dried thyme

- $\frac{1}{2}$ teaspoon salt

- $\frac{1}{4}$ teaspoon freshly ground black pepper

- 3 tablespoons olive oil

- Dijon mustard

- 4 whole grain burger rolls

- Sliced red onion, tomato, lettuce, and avocado

In a medium saucepan of simmering water, cook the tempeh for 30 minutes. Drain and set aside to cool.

In a food processor, combine the onion and garlic and process until minced. Add the cooled tempeh, the walnuts, oats, parsley, oregano, thyme, salt, and pepper. Process until well blended. Shape the mixture into 4 equal patties.

In a large skillet, heat the oil over medium heat. Add the burgers and cook until cooked thoroughly and browned on both sides, about 7 minutes per side.

Spread desired amount of mustard onto each half of the rolls and layer each roll with lettuce, tomato, red onion, and avocado, as desired. Serve immediately.

22.   Grilled Portobello Burgers

Makes 4 burgers

- 2 tablespoons olive oil

- 1 tablespoon balsamic vinegar

- $1/4$ teaspoon sugar

- $1/4$ teaspoon salt

- $1/8$ teaspoon freshly ground black pepper

- 4 large portobello mushroom caps, lightly rinsed and patted dry

- 4 slices red onion

- 4 kaiser rolls, halved horizontally or other burger rolls

- 8 large fresh basil leaves

- 4 slices ripe tomato

Preheat the grill or broiler. In a small bowl, combine the oil, vinegar, sugar, salt, and pepper. Set aside.

Place the mushroom caps and onion slices on the hot grill and cook until grilled on both sides, turning once, about 10 minutes total.

Brush the tops of the mushrooms and onion with the vinaigrette and keep warm. Place the rolls cut side down on the grill and lightly toast, about 1 minute.

Layer an onion slice and mushroom onto the bottom half of each roll. Top each with two basil leaves and a tomato slice. Drizzle with any remaining vinaigrette and cover each burger with the roll tops. Serve immediately.

23. Macadamia-Cashew Patties

Makes 4 patties

.

- 1 cup chopped macadamia nuts

- 1 cup chopped cashews

- 1 medium carrot, grated

- 1 small onion, chopped

- 1 garlic clove, minced

- 1 jalapeño or other green chile, seeded and minced

- 1 cup old-fashioned oats

- 1 cup dry unseasoned bread crumbs

- 2 tablespoons minced fresh cilantro

- $1/2$ teaspoon ground coriander

- Salt and freshly ground black pepper

- 2 teaspoons fresh lime juice

- Canola or grapeseed oil, for frying

- 4 sandwich rolls

- Lettuce leaves and condiment of choice (see headnote)

In a food processor, combine the macadamia nuts, cashews, carrot, onion, garlic, chile, oats, bread crumbs, cilantro, coriander, and salt and pepper to taste. Process until well mixed. Add the lime juice and process until well blended. Taste, adjusting seasonings if necessary. Shape the mixture into 4 equal patties.

In a large skillet, heat a thin layer of oil over medium heat. Add the patties and cook until golden brown on both sides, turning once, about 10 minutes total. Serve on sandwich rolls with lettuce and condiments of choice.

24.   Pecan-Lentil Burgers

Makes 4 to 6 burgers

- $1^1/_2$ cups cooked brown lentils

- $^1/_2$ cup ground pecans

- $^1/_2$ cup old-fashioned oats

- $^1/_4$ cup dry unseasoned bread crumbs

- $1/4$ cup wheat gluten flour (vital wheat gluten)

- $1/2$ cup minced onion

- $1/4$ cup minced fresh parsley

- 1 teaspoon Dijon mustard

- $1/2$ teaspoon salt

- $1/8$ teaspoon freshly ground pepper

- 2 tablespoons olive oil

- 4 to 6 burger rolls

- Lettuce leaves, sliced tomato, sliced red onion, and condiments of choice

In a food processor, combine the lentils, pecans, oats, bread crumbs, flour, onion, parsley, mustard, salt, and pepper. Pulse to combine, leaving some texture. Shape the lentil mixture into 4 to 6 burgers.

In a large skillet, heat the oil over medium heat. Add the burgers and cook until golden brown, about 5 minutes per side.

Serve the burgers on the rolls with lettuce, tomato slices, onion, and condiments of choice.

25. Black Bean Burgers

Makes 4 burgers

- 3 tablespoons olive oil

- $^1/_2$ cup minced onion

- 1 garlic clove, minced

- $1^1/_2$ cups cooked or 1 (15.5-ounce) can black beans, drained and rinsed

- 1 tablespoon minced fresh parsley

- $^1\!/_2$ cup dry unseasoned bread crumbs

- $^1\!/_4$ cup wheat gluten flour (vital wheat gluten)

- 1 teaspoon smoked paprika

- $^1\!/_2$ teaspoon dried thyme

- Salt and freshly ground black pepper

- 4 burger rolls

- 4 lettuce leaves

- 1 ripe tomato, cut into $^1\!/_4$-inch slices

In a small skillet, heat 1 tablespoon of the oil over medium heat. Add the onion and garlic and cook until softened, about 5 minutes.

Transfer the onion mixture to a food processor. Add the beans, parsley, bread crumbs, flour, paprika, thyme, and salt and pepper to taste. Process until well combined, leaving some texture. Shape the mixture into 4 equal patties and refrigerate for 20 minutes.

In a large skillet, heat the remaining 2 tablespoons oil over medium heat. Add the burgers and cook until browned on both sides, turning once, about 5 minutes per side.

Serve the burgers on the rolls with lettuce and tomato slices.

26.   Some-Kinda-Nut Burgers

Makes 4 burgers

- 2 tablespoons plus 1 teaspoon olive oil

- 1 small onion, chopped

- 1 medium carrot, grated

- 1 cup unsalted mixed nuts

- $1/4$ cup wheat gluten flour (vital wheat gluten), plus more if needed

- $1/2$ cup old-fashioned oats, plus more if needed

- 2 tablespoons creamy peanut butter

- 2 tablespoons minced fresh parsley

- $1/2$ teaspoon salt

- $1/4$ teaspoon freshly ground black pepper

- 4 burger rolls

- 4 lettuce leaves

- 1 ripe tomato, cut into $1/4$-inch slices

In a medium skillet, heat 1 teaspoon of the oil over medium heat. Add the onion and cook until soft, about 5 minutes. Stir in the carrot and set aside.

In a food processor, pulse the nuts until chopped. Add the onion-carrot mixture along with the flour, oats, peanut butter, parsley, salt, and pepper. Process until well blended. Shape the mixture into 4 equal patties, about 4 inches in diameter. If the mixture is too loose, add a little more flour or oats.

In a large skillet, heat the remaining 2 tablespoons oil over medium heat, add the burgers and cook until browned on both sides, about 5 minutes per side.

Serve the burgers on the rolls with lettuce and tomato slices.

27.   Golden Veggie Burgers

Makes 4 burgers

- 2 tablespoons olive oil

- 1 small yellow onion, chopped

- $1/2$ small yellow bell pepper, chopped

- $1^1/2$ cups cooked or 1 (15.5-ounce) can chickpeas, drained and rinsed

- $\frac{3}{4}$ teaspoon salt

- $1/4$ teaspoon freshly ground black pepper

- $1/4$ cup wheat gluten flour (vital wheat gluten)

- 4 burger rolls

- Condiments of choice

In a large skillet, heat 1 tablespoon of the oil over medium heat. Add the onion and pepper and cook until softened, about 5 minutes. Set aside to cool slightly.

Transfer the cooled onion mixture to a food processor. Add the chickpeas, salt, and black pepper and pulse to mix. Add the flour and process to combine.

Shape the mixture into 4 burgers, about 4 inches in diameter. If the mixture is too loose, add a little extra flour.

In a large skillet, heat the remaining 2 tablespoons of oil over medium heat. Add the burgers and cook until firm and browned on both sides, turning once, about 5 minutes per side.

Serve the burgers on the rolls with condiments of choice.

28.   Red Lentil Patties In Pita

Makes 4 pitas

- $^1/_2$ cup red lentils, picked over, rinsed, and drained

- 2 tablespoons olive oil

- $^1/_2$ cup minced onion

- 1 small potato, peeled and shredded

- $1/2$ cup roasted cashews

- $1/4$ cup chickpea flour or wheat gluten flour

- 1 tablespoon minced fresh parsley

- 2 teaspoons hot or mild curry powder

- $1/2$ teaspoon salt

- $1/8$ teaspoon ground cayenne

- 4 (7-inch) pita breads, warmed and halved

- Shredded romaine lettuce

- Fresh Mint and Coconut Chutney or your favorite chutney

Bring a small saucepan of salted water to boil over high heat. Add the lentils, return to a boil, then reduce heat to low. Cover and cook until tender, about 15 minutes. Drain well, then return to the saucepan and cook over low heat for 1 to 2 minutes, stirring, to evaporate any remaining moisture. Set aside.

In a large skillet, heat 1 tablespoon of the oil over medium heat. Add the onion and potato, cover, and cook until soft, about 5 minutes. Set aside.

In a food processor, process the cashews until finely ground. Add the cooked lentils and the

onion-potato mixture and pulse to combine. Add the flour, parsley, curry powder, salt, and cayenne.

Process until just mixed, leaving some texture. Shape the mixture into 8 small patties.

In a large skillet, heat the remaining 1 tablespoon of oil over medium heat. Add the patties and cook until browned on both sides, about 5 minutes per side.

Stuff a patty inside each pita half, along with some shredded lettuce and a spoonful of chutney. Serve immediately.

29.　White Bean And Walnut Patties

Makes 4 patties

- $^1/_4$ cup diced onion

- 1 garlic clove, crushed

- 1 cup walnut pieces

- 1 cup canned or cooked white beans, drained and rinsed

- 1 cup wheat gluten flour (vital wheat gluten)

- 2 tablespoons minced fresh parsley

- 1 tablespoon soy sauce

- 1 teaspoon Dijon mustard, plus more to serve

- $1/2$ teaspoon salt

- $1/2$ teaspoon ground sage

- $1/2$ teaspoon sweet paprika

- $1/4$ teaspoon turmeric

- $1/4$ teaspoon freshly ground black pepper

- 2 tablespoons olive oil

- Bread or rolls of choice

- Lettuce leaves and sliced tomatoes

In a food processor, combine the onion, garlic, and walnuts and process until finely ground.

Cook the beans in a small skillet over medium heat, stirring, for 1 to 2 minutes to evaporate any moisture. Add the beans to the food processor along with the flour, parsley, soy sauce, mustard, salt, sage, paprika, turmeric, and pepper. Process until well blended. Shape the mixture into 4 equal patties.

In a large skillet, heat the oil over medium heat. Add the patties and cook until browned on both sides, about 5 minutes per side.

Serve on your favorite sandwich bread with mustard, lettuce, and sliced tomatoes.

30.   Curried Chickpea Patties

Makes 4 patties

- 3 tablespoons olive oil

- 1 small onion, chopped

- $1^1/_2$ teaspoons hot or mild curry powder

- $^1/_2$ teaspoon salt

- $^1/_8$ teaspoon ground cayenne

- 1 cup cooked chickpeas

- 1 tablespoon chopped fresh parsley

- $^1/_2$ cup wheat gluten flour (vital wheat gluten)

- $^1/_3$ cup dry unseasoned bread crumbs

- $^1/_4$ cup vegan mayonnaise, homemade (see Vegan Mayonnaise) or store-bought

- Bread or rolls of choice

- Lettuce leaves

- 1 ripe tomato, cut into $^1/_4$-inch slices

In a large skillet, heat 1 tablespoon of the oil over medium heat. Add the onion, cover, and cook until softened, 5 minutes. Stir in 1 teaspoon of the curry powder, salt, and cayenne and remove from the heat. Set aside.

In a food processor, combine the chickpeas, parsley, wheat gluten flour, bread crumbs, and the cooked onion. Process to combine, leaving some texture.

Form the chickpea mixture into 4 equal patties and set aside.

In a large skillet, heat the remaining 2 tablespoons oil over medium heat. Add the patties, cover, and cook until golden brown on both sides, turning once, about 5 minutes per side.

In a small bowl, combine the remaining $\frac{1}{2}$ teaspoon of curry powder with the mayonnaise, stirring

to blend. Spread the curried mayonnaise on the bread. Top with the patties, lettuce, and tomato slices. Serve immediately.

31.   Pinto Bean Patties With Mayo

Makes 4 patties

- $1^1/_2$ cups cooked or 1 (15.5-ounce) can pinto beans, rinsed and drained

- 1 medium shallot, chopped

- 1 garlic clove, minced

- 2 tablespoons chopped fresh cilantro

- 1 teaspoon Creole seasoning

- $1/4$ cup wheat gluten flour (vital wheat gluten)

- Salt and freshly ground black pepper

- $1/2$ cup dry unseasoned bread crumbs

- 1 cup vegan mayonnaise, homemade (see Vegan Mayonnaise) or store-bought

- 2 teaspoons fresh lime juice

- 1 serrano chile, seeded and minced

- 2 tablespoons olive oil

- Bread, flour tortillas, or sandwich rolls

- Shredded lettuce

- 1 tomato, cut into $1/4$-inch slices

Blot the beans with paper towels to absorb excess moisture. In a food processor, combine the beans, shallot, garlic, cilantro, Creole seasoning, flour, and salt and pepper to taste. Process until well blended.

Shape the mixture into 4 equal patties, adding more flour if needed. Dredge the patties in the bread crumbs. Refrigerate for 20 minutes.

In a small bowl, combine the mayonnaise, lime juice, and serrano chile. Season with the salt and pepper to taste, mix well, and refrigerate until ready to serve.

In a large skillet, heat the oil over medium heat. Add the patties and cook until browned and crispy on both sides, about 5 minutes per side.

Spread the chile-lime mayo on the bread and top with the patties, lettuce, and tomato. Serve immediately.

FAJITAS AND BURRITOS

32.   Seared Portobello Fajitas

Makes 4 fajitas

- 2 tablespoons olive oil

- 3 large portobello mushroom caps, lightly rinsed, patted dry, and cut into $1/4$-inch strips
- 1 serrano or other hot chile, seeded and minced (optional)

- 3 cups fresh baby spinach

- $1/4$ teaspoon ground cumin

- $1/4$ teaspoon dried oregano

- Salt and freshly ground black pepper

- 4 (10-inch) flour tortillas, warmed

- 1 cup tomato salsa, homemade (see Fresh Tomato Salsa) or store-bought

In a large skillet, heat the oil over medium high heat. Add the mushrooms, onion, and chile, if using, and cook until seared on the outside and slightly softened, stirring occasionally, about 5 minutes.

Add the spinach and cook until wilted, 1 to 2 minutes. Season with the cumin, oregano, and salt and pepper to taste.

To assemble the fajitas, place 1 tortilla on a work surface. Spread with one-quarter of the mushroom mixture. Spoon $1/4$ cup of the salsa on top and roll up tightly. Repeat with remaining ingredients. Serve immediately.

33.   Beer-Marinated Seitan Fajitas

Makes 4 fajitas

- $^1/_2$ cup chopped red onion

- 1 garlic clove, minced

- $^1/_2$ cup beer

- 2 teaspoons fresh lime juice

- 1 tablespoon chopped fresh cilantro

- $1/4$ teaspoon crushed red pepper

- $1/2$ teaspoon salt

- 8 ounces seitan, homemade (see Basic Simmered Seitan) or store-bought, cut into $1/4$-inch strips

- 2 tablespoons olive oil

- 1 ripe Hass avocado

- 4 (10-inch) flour tortillas, warmed

- $1/2$ cup tomato salsa, homemade (see Fresh Tomato Salsa) or store-bought

In a shallow bowl, combine the onion, garlic, beer, lime juice, cilantro, crushed red pepper, and salt. Add the seitan and marinate for 4 hours or overnight in the refrigerator.

Remove the seitan from the marinade, reserving the marinade. In a large skillet, heat the oil over medium heat. Add the seitan and cook until browned on both sides, about 10 minutes. Add the reserved marinade and simmer until most of the liquid is evaporated.

Pit, peel, and cut the avocado into $1/2$-inch slices. To assemble the fajitas, place 1 tortilla on a

work surface and top with one-quarter of the seitan strips, salsa, and avocado slices. Roll up tightly and repeat with the remaining ingredients. Serve immediately.

34. Seitan Tacos

Makes 4 tacos

- 2 tablespoons olive oil

- 12 ounces seitan, homemade (see Basic Simmered Seitan) or store-bought, finely chopped

- 2 tablespoons soy sauce

- $1^1/_2$ teaspoons chili powder

- $^1/_4$ teaspoon ground cumin

- $^1/_4$ teaspoon garlic powder

- 12 (6-inch) soft corn tortillas

- 1 ripe Hass avocado

- Shredded romaine lettuce

- 1 cup tomato salsa, homemade (see Fresh Tomato Salsa) or store-bought

In a large skillet, heat the oil over medium heat. Add the seitan and cook until browned, about 10 minutes. Sprinkle with the soy sauce, chili powder, cumin, and garlic powder, stirring to coat. Remove from heat.

Preheat the oven to 225°F. In a medium skillet, warm the tortillas over medium heat and stack them on a heatproof plate. Cover with foil and place them in the oven to keep them soft and warm.

Pit and peel the avocado and cut into $1/4$-inch slices. Arrange the taco filling, avocado, and lettuce on a platter and serve along with the warmed tortillas, salsa, and any additional toppings.

35.   Bean and Salsa Quesadillas

Makes 4 quesadillas

- 1 tablespoon canola or grapeseed oil, plus more for frying

- $1^1/_2$ cups cooked or 1 (15.5-ounce) can pinto beans, drained and mashed

- 1 teaspoon chili powder

- 4 (10-inch) flour tortillas

- 1 cup tomato salsa, homemade (see Fresh Tomato Salsa) or store-bought

In a medium saucepan, heat the oil over medium heat. Add the mashed beans and chili powder and cook, stirring, until hot, about 5 minutes. Set aside.

To assemble, place 1 tortilla on a work surface and spoon about $1/4$ cup of the beans across the

bottom half. Top the beans with the salsa and onion, if using. Fold top half of the tortilla over the filling and press slightly.

In large skillet heat a thin layer of oil over medium heat. Place folded quesadillas, 1 or 2 at a time, into the hot skillet and heat until hot, turning once, about 1 minute per side.

Cut quesadillas into 3 or 4 wedges and arrange on plates. Serve immediately.

36.   Spinach and Black Bean Quesadillas

Makes 4 quesadillas

- $1^1/_2$ cups cooked or 1 (15.5 ounce) can black beans, drained and rinsed

- 1 tablespoon olive oil

- $^1/_2$ cup minced red onion

- 2 garlic cloves, minced

- 2 cups sliced white mushrooms

- 4 cups fresh baby spinach

- Salt and freshly ground black pepper

- 4 (10-inch) flour tortillas

- Canola or grapeseed oil, for frying

Place the black beans in a medium bowl and coarsely mash them. Set aside.

In a small skillet, heat the olive oil over medium heat. Add the onion and garlic and cover and cook until softened, about 5 minutes. Stir in the mushrooms and cook, uncovered, until softened. Add the spinach, season with salt and pepper to taste, and cook, stirring, until the spinach is wilted, about 3 minutes.

Stir in the mashed black beans and continue cooking, stirring, until liquid is absorbed.

To assemble quesadillas, place 1 tortilla at a time on a work surface and spoon about one-quarter mixture onto the bottom half of the tortilla. Fold the top half of the tortillas over the filling and press lightly.

In a large skillet, heat a thin layer of oil over medium heat. Place the folded quesadillas, 1 or 2 at a time, into the hot skillet and heat over medium heat until hot, turning once, about 1 minute per side.

Cut the quesadillas into 3 or 4 wedges each and arrange on plates. Serve immediately.

37.　Black Bean And Corn Burritos

Makes 4 burritos

- 1 tablespoon olive oil

- $^1/_2$ cup chopped onion

- $1^1/_2$ cups cooked or 1 (15.5-ounce) can black beans, drained and rinsed
- $^1/_2$ cup tomato salsa, homemade (see Fresh Tomato Salsa) or store-bought

- 4 (10-inch) flour tortillas, warmed

In a saucepan, heat the oil over medium heat. Add the onion, cover, and cook until softened, about 5 minutes. Add the beans and mash them until broken up.

Add the corn and salsa, stirring to combine. Simmer, stirring, until the bean mixture is hot about 5 minutes.

To assemble burritos, place 1 tortilla on a work surface and spoon about $^1/_2$ cup of the filling

mixture down the center. Roll up tightly, tucking in the sides. Repeat with the remaining ingredients. Serve seam side down.

38.   Red Bean Burritos

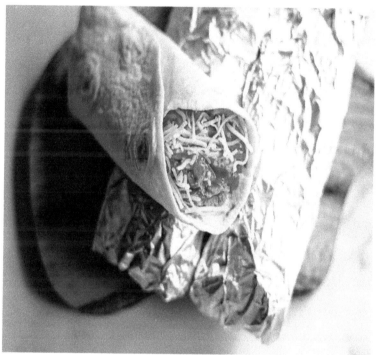

Makes 4 burritos

- 1 tablespoon olive oil

- 1 medium onion, chopped

- 1 medium red bell pepper, chopped

- $1^1/_2$ cups cooked or 1 (15.5-ounce) can dark red kidney beans, drained and rinsed

- 1 cup tomato salsa, homemade (see Fresh Tomato Salsa) or store-bought, plus extra if desired

- 4 (10-inch) flour tortillas, warmed

- 1 cup hot cooked rice

- 1 ripe Hass avocado, pitted, peeled, and cut into $1/_4$-inch slices

In a medium saucepan, heat the oil over medium heat. Add the onion and bell pepper, cover, and cook until softened, about 5 minutes. Add the beans and salsa and cook, stirring to combine. Simmer, mashing the beans as you stir them, until hot.

To assemble burritos, place 1 tortillas on a work surface and spoon about $1/_2$ cup of the bean

mixture down the center. Top with the rice, followed by slices of avocado and extra salsa, if desired. Roll up tightly, tucking in the sides. Repeat with the remaining ingredients. Serve seam-side down.

PIZZA, CALZONE, STROMBOLI, AND TURNOVERS

39.   Basic Pizza Dough

Makes one 12-inch pizza

- Olive oil

- 1 cup warm water

- 1 ($^1/_4$ ounce) packet active dry yeast ($2^1/_4$ teaspoons)

- $1^1/_4$ teaspoons salt

- Pinch sugar

- $2^1/_2$ cups all-purpose flour, plus more as needed

Lightly oil a medium bowl and set aside. In a separate medium bowl, combine the warm water and yeast. Stir until yeast is dissolved.

Add the salt, sugar, and flour, and mix just long enough to form a soft dough. Add small additional amounts of flour if the dough is too sticky. Do not overmix.

With well-floured hands, place the dough into the oiled bowl, turning the dough to coat with oil. Cover with plastic wrap or a clean kitchen towel. Let the dough rise in a warm spot until doubled in bulk, about 1 hour.

40.   Vegan Margherita Pizza

Makes 4 servings

- 1 recipe Basic Pizza Dough

- 1 cup firm tofu, drained

- 1 tablespoon nutritional yeast

- 2 ripe plum tomatoes, sliced paper thin

- 11/2 tablespoons olive oil

- 1/4 cup vegan basil pesto, homemade (see Basil Pistou) or store-bought, room temperature Salt and freshly ground black pepper

Flatten the risen dough slightly, cover with plastic wrap or a clean towel, and set aside to relax for 10 minutes.

Place the oven rack on the lowest level of the oven. Preheat the oven to 450°F. Lightly oil a pizza pan or large baking sheet.

Turn the relaxed dough out onto a lightly floured surface and flatten with your hands, turning and flouring frequently, working it into a 12-inch round. Be careful not to overwork the middle or the center of the crust will be too thin. Transfer the dough to the prepared pizza pan or baking sheet.

In a food processor, combine the tofu and nutritional yeast and process until smooth. Add salt and pepper to taste and blend until smooth. Set aside.

Blot any excess liquid from the tomato slices with paper towels.

Spread $1/2$ tablespoon of the olive oil onto the prepared pizza dough, using your fingertips to spread evenly. Top with the tofu mixture, spreading evenly to about $1/2$ inch from the dough's edge.

Whisk the remaining 1 tablespoon of oil into the pesto and spread evenly over the tofu mixture to about $1/2$ inch from the dough's edge. Arrange the tomato slices on the pizza and season with salt and pepper to taste.

Bake until the crust is golden brown, about 12 minutes. Cut the pizza into 8 wedges and serve hot.

41.   Portobello And Black Olive Pizza

Makes 4 servings

- 1 recipe Basic Pizza Dough

- 2 tablespoons olive oil

- 2 portobello mushroom caps, lightly rinsed, patted dry, and cut into $1/4$-inch slices

- 1 tablespoon finely chopped fresh basil

- $1/4$ teaspoon dried oregano

- Salt and freshly ground black pepper
- $1/2$ cup pizza sauce or marinara sauce (see Marinara Sauce)

Flatten the risen dough slightly, cover with plastic wrap or a clean dish towel, and set aside to relax for 10 minutes.

Place the oven rack on the lowest level of the oven. Preheat the oven to 450°F. Lightly oil a pizza pan or large baking sheet.

Turn the relaxed dough out onto a lightly floured work surface and flatten with your hands, turning and flouring frequently, working it into a 12-inch round. Be careful not to overwork the middle or the center of the crust will be too thin. Transfer the dough to the prepared pizza pan or baking sheet.

In a large skillet, heat 1 tablespoon of the oil over medium heat. Add the mushrooms and cook until softened, about 5 minutes. Remove from heat and add the basil, oregano, and salt and pepper to taste. Stir in the olives and set aside.

Spread the remaining 1 tablespoon oil onto the prepared pizza dough, using your fingertips to spread it evenly. Top with the pizza sauce, spreading evenly to about $1/2$ inch from the dough's edge. Spread the vegetable mixture evenly over the sauce, to about $1/2$ inch from the dough's edge.

Bake until the crust is golden brown, about 12 minutes. Cut the pizza into 8 wedges and serve hot.

Makes 4 servings

- 1 recipe Basic Pizza Dough

- 2 tablespoons olive oil

- $^1/_2$ cup thinly sliced red onion

- $^1/_4$ cup chopped red bell pepper

- 1 cup sliced white mushrooms

- $^1/_2$ cup pizza sauce or marinara sauce, homemade (see Marinara Sauce) or store-bought

- $^1/_4$ teaspoon dried basil

- Salt and freshly ground black pepper

- 2 tablespoons sliced pitted kalamata olives

- Optional toppings: sautéed zucchini, sliced hot peppers, artichoke hearts, sun-dried tomatoes

Place the oven rack on the lowest level of the oven. Preheat the oven to 450°F. Lightly oil a pizza pan or large baking sheet.

Once the pizza dough has risen, flatten the dough slightly, cover with plastic wrap or a clean towel, and set aside to relax for 10 minutes.

Turn the dough out onto a floured surface and use your hands to flatten it, turning and flouring frequently, working it into a 12-inch round. Be careful not to overwork the middle or the center of the crust will be too thin. Transfer the dough to the prepared pizza pan or baking sheet.

In a large skillet, heat 1 tablespoon of the oil over medium heat. Add the onion, bell pepper, and mushrooms and cook until softened, about 5 minutes. Remove from heat and set aside.

Spread the remaining 1 tablespoon of oil onto the prepared pizza dough, using your fingertips to spread it evenly. Top with the pizza sauce, spreading evenly to about $1/2$ inch from the dough's edge. Sprinkle with the oregano and basil.

Spread the vegetable mixture evenly over the sauce to within about $1/2$ inch from the dough's edge. Season with salt and black pepper to taste. Sprinkle with the olives and any desired toppings. Bake until the crust is golden brown, about 12 minutes. Cut the pizza into 8 wedges and serve hot.

43.   White Pizza With And Yellow Tomatoes

Makes 4 servings

- 1 medium Yukon Gold potato, peeled and cut into $1/4$-inch slices

- Salt and freshly ground black pepper

- 1 recipe Basic Pizza Dough

- 2 tablespoons olive oil

- 1 medium Vidalia or other sweet onion, cut into $1/4$-inch slices

- 6 to 8 fresh basil leaves

- 2 ripe yellow tomatoes, cut into $1/4$-inch slices

Place the oven rack on the lowest level of the oven. Preheat the oven to 450°F. Arrange the potato slices on a lightly oiled baking sheet and season with salt and pepper to taste. Bake until soft and golden brown, about 10 minutes. Set aside. Lightly oil a pizza pan or large baking sheet.

Once the pizza dough has risen, flatten the dough slightly, cover with plastic wrap or a clean towel, and set aside to relax for 10 minutes.

Turn the relaxed dough out onto a lightly floured surface and flatten with your hands, turning and flouring frequently, working it into a 12-inch round. Be careful not to overwork the middle or the center of the crust will be too thin. Transfer the dough to the prepared pizza pan or baking sheet.

In a large skillet, heat 1 tablespoon of the oil over medium heat. Add the onion and cook until soft and caramelized, stirring frequently, about 30 minutes. Remove from heat, season with oregano and salt and pepper to taste, and set aside.

Spread the remaining 1 tablespoon of olive oil onto the prepared pizza dough, using your fingertips to spread it evenly. Top with the caramelized onion, spreading evenly to about $^1/_2$ inch
from the dough's edge. Top with the basil leaves, then arrange the potato and tomato slices on top of the onions and basil.

Bake until the crust is golden brown, about 12 minutes. Cut the pizza into 8 wedges and serve hot.

44.   Spicy Southwestern Pizza

Makes 4 servings

- 1 recipe Basic Pizza Dough

- 1 tablespoon olive oil

- 1 teaspoon chili powder

- $1^1/_2$ cups cooked or 1 (15.5-ounce) can pinto beans, drained

- 1 cup tomato salsa, homemade (see Fresh Tomato Salsa) or store-bought

- 2 tablespoons hot or mild canned minced green chiles

- 2 tablespoons sliced pitted kalamata olives

- 2 tablespoons minced fresh cilantro

Flatten the risen dough slightly, cover with plastic wrap or a clean dish towel, and set aside to relax for 10 minutes.

Place the oven rack on the lowest level of them oven. Preheat the oven to 450°F. Lightly oil a pizza pan or large baking sheet. Turn the relaxed dough out onto a lightly floured surface and flatten with your hands, turning and flouring frequently, working it into a 12-inch round. Be careful not to overwork the middle or the center of the crust will be too thin. Transfer the dough to the prepared pizza pan or baking sheet.

In a medium saucepan, heat the oil over medium heat. Stir in the chili powder, then add the beans, stirring to combine and warm the beans, about 5 minutes.

Remove from the heat and mash the beans well, adding a small amount of the salsa, if needed, to moisten the beans.

Spread the bean mixture evenly onto the prepared pizza dough to about $^1/_2$ inch from the dough's edge. Spread the salsa evenly over the bean mixture and sprinkle with the chiles and olives.

Bake until the crust is golden brown, about 12 minutes. After removing the pizza from the oven, sprinkle with the cilantro, cut into 8 wedges, and serve hot.

45. Tapenade And Tomato Pizza

Makes 4 servings

- 1 recipe Basic Pizza Dough

- 3 ripe plum tomatoes, sliced paper thin

- 2 tablespoons olive oil

- $1/4$ cup black and green olive tapenade, homemade (see Black And Green Olive Tapenade) or store-bought

- 2 teaspoons capers, drained and chopped if large

Flatten the risen dough slightly, cover with plastic wrap or a clean dish towel, and set aside to relax for 10 minutes.

Place the oven rack on the lowest level of the oven. Preheat the oven to 450°F. Lightly oil a pizza pan or large baking sheet. Turn the relaxed dough out onto a lightly floured work surface and flatten with your hands, turning and flouring frequently, working it into a 12-inch round. Be careful not to overwork the middle or the center of the crust will be too thin. Transfer the dough to the prepared pizza pan or baking sheet.

Blot any excess liquid from the tomatoes with paper towels. Spread 1 tablespoon of the oil onto the prepared pizza dough, using your fingertips to spread it evenly.

Whisk the remaining 1 tablespoon of oil into the tapenade and spread the tapenade onto the pizza dough. Arrange the tomato slices on the pizza and sprinkle with the olives and capers.

Bake until the crust is golden brown, about 12 minutes. Cut into 8 wedges and serve hot.

46.   Mushroom and Pepper Calzones

Makes 4 calzones

- 1 recipe Basic Pizza Dough

- 1 tablespoon olive oil

- 3 garlic cloves, minced

- 1 pound white mushrooms, lightly rinsed, patted, dry, and chopped
- 8 ounces extra-firm tofu, drained and crumbled

- $1/2$ teaspoon dried oregano

- 1 teaspoon salt

- $1/4$ teaspoon freshly ground black pepper

Flatten the risen dough slightly, cover with plastic wrap or clean dish towel, and set aside to relax for 10 minutes.

Preheat the oven to 400°F. In a large skillet, heat the oil over medium heat. Add the garlic and cook until fragrant, about 30 seconds. Add the mushrooms and cook, stirring, until any liquid evaporates, about 5 minutes. Chop the cherry peppers and add to the mushrooms along with the tofu, oregano, salt, and pepper. Cook stirring to blend the flavors and evaporate any remaining liquid, about 5 minutes. Remove from the heat and set aside to cool.

Turn the relaxed dough out onto a lightly floured work surface and divide into 4 equal pieces. Use your hands to flatten each piece into 6-inch circles, turning and flouring as needed.

Divide the filling equally among the dough circles, leaving a $1/2$-inch border. Fold each dough circle over the filling to meet the opposite edge of the dough.

With dampened fingers, press the edges of the dough together to seal the filling inside.

Transfer the calzones to the prepared pizza pan or baking sheet and bake until golden brown, about 20 minutes.

If cherry peppers are unavailable, substitute another type of mild or hot jarred chile peppers or sauté one or two chopped fresh hot chiles with a chopped bell pepper.

47. Roasted Vegetable Stromboli

Makes 4 to 6 servings

- 1 recipe Basic Pizza Dough

- 1 medium red onion, chopped

- 1 medium red or yellow bell pepper, chopped

- 1 medium zucchini, chopped

- 2 garlic cloves, minced

- 8 ounces white mushrooms, lightly rinsed, patted dry, and cut into $1/4$-inch slices

- 3 ripe plum tomatoes, chopped

- 1 tablespoon minced fresh basil

- $1/2$ teaspoon dried oregano

- $1/4$ teaspoon crushed red pepper (optional)

- Salt and freshly ground black pepper

- 2 tablespoons olive oil

- $1/2$ cup pizza sauce or marinara sauce, homemade (see Marinara Sauce) or store-bought

- 2 tablespoons vegan Parmesan cheese or Parmasio

Make the dough. Preheat the oven to 450°F.

In a lightly oiled shallow baking pan, combine the onion, bell pepper, zucchini, garlic, mushrooms, tomatoes, basil, oregano, crushed red pepper, if using, and salt and black pepper to taste. Drizzle with the olive oil, stirring to coat the vegetables.

Place the baking pan in the oven and roast the vegetables until tender, stirring occasionally, 20 to 30 minutes. Remove from the oven and set aside to cool. Drain the vegetables and blot them dry.

Reduce the oven temperature to 375°F. Lightly oil a large baking sheet and set aside.

Punch down the dough down and divide it in half. Turn one of the dough pieces out onto a lightly floured surface and flatten with your hands, turning and flouring frequently, working it into a 9 x 12-inch rectangle.

Add the pizza sauce to the vegetable mixture, stirring to combine. Sprinkle with the Parmesan, if using.

Spread half of the cooled vegetable mixture across the dough leaving a 1-inch border on all sides.

Beginning at a long side, roll the stromboli into a cylinder, pinching the edges to seal in the filling.

Transfer the stromboli to the prepared baking sheet, seam side down. Repeat with the remaining ingredients.

Bake until the crust is golden brown, about 30 minutes. Remove from the oven and let stand 10 minutes. Use a serrated knife to cut into thick slices and serve.

48.   Spicy Tempeh Empanadas

Makes 6 empanadas

- 8 ounces tempeh

- 2 tablespoons olive oil

- 1 medium yellow onion, finely chopped

- 2 garlic cloves, minced

- $1/2$ teaspoon dried oregano

- $1/2$ teaspoon ground cumin

- $1/2$ teaspoon crushed red pepper

- $1^1/2$ teaspoons salt

- $1/4$ teaspoon black pepper

- $1/2$ cup ketchup

- $1/2$ cup raisins

- $1/4$ cup fresh orange juice

- $1^1/2$ cups all-purpose flour

- $1/2$ cup yellow or white cornmeal

- 1 teaspoon sugar

- 1 teaspoon baking powder

- $1/2$ cup vegan margarine

- $1/3$ cup plus 2 teaspoons soy milk

- 2 teaspoons Dijon mustard

In a medium saucepan of simmering water, cook the tempeh for 30 minutes. Drain well, chop, and set aside.

In a large skillet, heat the oil over medium heat, add onion and garlic, cover, and cook until softened, 5 minutes.

Stir in the chopped tempeh, oregano, cumin, crushed red pepper, the $1/2$ teaspoon salt, and black

pepper. Cook 5 minutes longer, then reduce the heat to low and stir in the ketchup, raisins, and orange juice. Simmer until flavors have blended and liquid has evaporated, about 15 minutes. Set aside to cool.

Preheat the oven to 400°F. In a food processor, combine the flour, cornmeal, sugar, the remaining 1 teaspoon salt, and baking powder. Pulse to blend. Add the margarine, soy milk, and mustard. Process until a soft dough forms.

Divide the dough into 6 equal pieces and roll them out into 7-inch circles on a lightly floured work surface.

Divide the filling mixture onto one half of each dough circle. Fold the other half of the dough over the filling and crimp the edges to seal the filling inside.

Bake until golden brown, 25 to 30 minutes. Serve hot.

49. Quick Pinto-Potato Empanadas

Makes 4 empanadas

- $1^1/_2$ cups cooked or 1 (15.5-ounce) can pinto beans, drained and rinsed

- 1 small baked russet potato, peeled and coarsely chopped

- $^1/_2$ cup tomato salsa, homemade (see Fresh Tomato Salsa) or store-bought

- $1/2$ teaspoon chili powder

- $1/2$ teaspoon salt

- $1/4$ teaspoon freshly ground black pepper

- 1 sheet frozen puff pastry, thawed

Preheat the oven to 400°F. In a medium bowl, mash the beans slightly with a fork. Add the potato, salsa, chili powder, salt, and pepper. Mash well and set aside.

Roll out the pastry on a lightly floured board and divide into quarters.

Spoon the bean mixture onto the four pieces of dough, dividing evenly. For each empanada, fold one end of the dough over the filling to meet the opposite end of the dough. Use your fingers to seal and crimp the edges to enclose the filling. Use a fork to pierce the top of empanadas and place them on an ungreased baking sheet.

Bake until golden brown, about 20 minutes.

50.   Lentil Walnut Pasties

Makes 4 to 6 pasties

- 2 cups all-purpose flour

- $1^1/_2$ teaspoons baking powder

- $1^1/_2$ teaspoons salt

- $^2/_3$ cup vegan margarine, softened

- $1/3$ cup soy milk

- 1 tablespoon olive oil

- 1 small potato, peeled and shredded

- 1 medium carrot, finely chopped

- $1/2$ cup minced onion

- 2 garlic cloves, minced

- 1 teaspoon soy sauce

- $1/2$ teaspoon dried thyme

- $1/2$ teaspoon dried savoury

- $1/4$ teaspoon freshly ground black pepper

- 1 cup cooked brown lentils

- $1/2$ cup finely chopped walnuts

In a large bowl, combine the flour, baking powder, and 1 teaspoon of the salt. Use a pastry blender or fork to cut in the margarine until the mixture resembles coarse crumbs. Slowly stir in the soy milk, adding just enough to form a dough.

Wrap the dough in plastic wrap and refrigerate for 20 minutes. Preheat the oven to 375°F. Grease a baking sheet and set aside.

In a large skillet, heat the oil over medium heat. Add the potato, carrot, onion, garlic, soy sauce, thyme, savory, pepper, and remaining $1/2$ teaspoon salt. Cover and cook until the vegetables are soft, about 10 minutes. Stir in the cooked lentils and the walnuts and set aside.

Roll the chilled dough out on a lightly floured work surface until about $1/8$ inch thick and use a 4-

inch round cookie cutter (or the rim of a 4-inch bowl or glass) to cut the dough into four 4-inch circles.

Place about $3/4$ cup of the filling in the canter of each dough circle. Overlap the dough and pinch the edges together to form a half circle. Roll up the ends to make a smooth edge.

Place the pasties on the prepared baking sheet.
Brush with a little oil and bake until golden brown,

about 20 minutes. Serve hot.

51.   Mushroom Turnovers

Makes 4 turnovers

- 1 tablespoon olive oil

- 1 small onion, minced

- 1 garlic clove, minced

- 3 cups sliced white mushrooms

- $^1/_2$ teaspoon dried thyme

- $^1/_2$ teaspoon dried savory

- $^1/_8$ teaspoon ground cayenne

- $^1/_2$ cup frozen peas, thawed

- 1/2 cup vegan sour cream, home-made (see Tofu Sour Cream) or store-bought, or pureed tofu Salt and freshly ground black pepper

- 1 sheet frozen puff pastry, thawed

- 1 tablespoon soy milk

Preheat the oven to 425°F. In a large skillet, heat the oil over medium heat. Add the onion and garlic and cook until softened, about 5 minutes. Stir in the mushrooms, thyme, savory, and cayenne. Cover and cook until just tender, about 5 minutes.

Uncover and continue to cook until the liquid has evaporated. Remove from the heat and set aside to cool. Stir in the peas and sour cream and season to taste with salt and pepper. Set aside.

Roll out the pastry and divide into quarters. Spoon the mushroom mixture into the center of each piece of pastry, dividing evenly.

Fold the pastry in half over the filling to enclose the filling. Use your fingers to press the edges together to seal the filling inside.

Brush each turnover with soy milk and pierce the top with a fork. Bake until golden brown, 15 to 20 minutes. Serve warm.

52.   Indian-Style Pizza

Makes 2 servings

- 1 cup vegan plain yogurt

- 1 cup semolina flour

- 1 tablespoon cornstarch

- 1/3 cup plus 2 tablespoons water

- 1 medium carrot, grated

- 1 hot or mild green chile, seeded and finely minced

- 1/4 cup plus 1 tablespoon chopped fresh cilantro

- 1/4 cup finely chopped unsalted cashews

- 1 teaspoon ground coriander
- 1/2 teaspoon salt

- 2 tablespoons canola or grapeseed oil

Place the yogurt in a medium bowl and warm it in the microwave for 30 seconds. Stir in the flour and mix well to combine.

In a small bowl, combine the cornstarch with the 2 tablespoons of water. Blend well, then stir it into the flour mixture, adding the remaining $1/3$ cup of water to form a thick batter.

Stir in the carrot, chile, onion, the $1/4$ cup of cilantro, cashews, coriander, and salt, blending well. Set aside for 20 minutes at room temperature. Preheat the oven to 250°F.

In a large skillet, heat the oil over medium heat. Pour half of the batter into the skillet. Cover and cook until the bottom is lightly browned and the batter is cooked through, about 5 minutes. Be careful not to burn.

Carefully slide the uttapam onto a baking sheet or heatproof platter and keep warm while you cook the second one with the remaining batter.

Invert each uttappam onto dinner plates, sprinkle with the remaining 1 tablespoon cilantro, and serve hot.

CONCLUSION

Aren't fast foods awesome? They're convenient, your hands stay clean (for the most part!), and you pretty much have an infinite number of variations. Different breads, fillings, sauces, the list goes on and on, literally.

Of course, sandwiches and burgers aren't just for eating at home. Part of their convenience is having the ability of packing them up and taking them anywhere, work, picnic or simply a day out where you want to take your own food with you.

However, there are consequences to eating junk food- today; more than half of adults are considered overweight, with around 25% of the adult population defined as clinically obese.

That's right. Ultimately, it's up to us to eat better. And that's why, with the recipes in this book you get vegan junk food that are way healthier, animal-free and even more flavorful. Enjoy!

CPSIA information can be obtained
at www.ICGtesting.com
Printed in the USA
BVHW090140260521
608098BV00012B/2231

9 781802 881790